How to Study the Bible

Jack Kuhatschek

InterVarsity Press
P.O. Box 1400, Downers Grove, IL 60515-1426
ivpress.com
email@ivpress.com

InterVarsity Press® is the book-publishing division of InterVarsity Christian Fellowship/USA®, a movement of students and faculty active on campus at hundreds of universities, colleges and schools of nursing in the United States of America, and a member movement of the International Fellowship of Evangelical Students. For information about local and regional activities, visit intervarsity.org.

All Scripture quotations, unless otherwise indicated, are taken from the Holy Bible, New International Version®. NIV®. *Copyright ©1973, 1978, 1984 by International Bible Society. Used by permission of Zondervan Publishing House. All rights reserved.*

ISBN 978-0-87784-074-9

Printed in the United States of America ∞

P	28	27	26	25	24	23	22	21	20	19	18
Y	26	25	24	23	22	21	20	19	18	17	16

Several years ago the *New York Times* ran an advertisement of Mortimer Adler's *How to Read a Book*. Under the picture of a puzzled adolescent reading a letter were these words:

How to Read a Love Letter

This young man has just received his first love letter. He may have read it three or four times, but he is just beginning. To read it as accurately as he would like, would require several dictionaries and a good deal of close work with a few experts of etymology and philology. However, he will do all right without them.

He will ponder over the exact shade of meaning of every word, every comma. She has headed the letter, "Dear John." What, he asks himself, is the exact significance of those words? Did she refrain from saying "Dearest" because she was bashful? Would "My Dear" have sounded too formal?

Jeepers, maybe she would have said "Dear So-and-So" to anybody! A worried frown will now appear on his face. But it disappears as soon as he really gets to thinking about the first sentence. She certainly wouldn't have written *that* to anybody!

And so he works his way through the letter, one moment perched blissfully on a cloud, the next moment huddled miserably behind an eight-ball. It has started a hundred questions in his mind. He could quote it by heart. In fact, he will—to himself—for weeks to come.

The advertisement concludes: "If people read books with anything like the same concentration, we'd be a race of mental giants."[1]

The Bible is God's love letter to us. But if we want to experience the eagerness and intensity of the young man in the advertisement, we must learn how to study it on our own. This booklet presents the basic skills needed for studying the Bible. These skills are vitally important for both new Christians and those who have known Christ for many years.

The Nature of Scripture

The Bible is unique. It is unlike any other book because God himself is the Author. Because the Bible is God's book, it is *eternal*—it speaks to people in every time, place, language and culture. It never loses its relevance; it is never out of date.

In another sense the Bible is not unique. Because it was also written by human authors, the Bible shares many similarities with other books. Like other nonfiction books the Bible is *historical*—it was first written to people in a particular time, place, language and culture. And like other books the Bible is *literature*—the authors communicated through stories, poems, letters and parables.

The historical, literary and eternal qualities of Scripture require us to follow three steps in studying and applying the Bible:

First, if we take the historical nature of Scripture seriously, we must learn something about the time, language, culture and geography of the biblical world. This will help us understand how God's Word spoke to those who first heard it.

Second, if we take the literary nature of Scripture seriously, we must acquire reading skills—the kind of skills required to understand any book. This will help us to understand what the author is saying.

Third, if we take the eternal nature of Scripture seriously, we will study the Bible carefully and prayerfully. This will help us to understand how God's Word speaks to us today.

Step One: Journeying into the Past

In 1895 H. G. Wells wrote a book called *The Time Machine*. In it he describes a machine that could transport a person into the past or future:

"Now I want you clearly to understand that this lever, being pressed over, sends the machine gliding into the future, and this other one reverses the motion. This saddle is the seat of the time traveller. Presently I am going to press the lever, and off the machine will go. It will vanish . . ." We all saw the lever turn. I am absolutely certain there was no trickery. There was a breath of wind, and the lamp flame jumped. One of the candles on the mantel was blown out, and the machine suddenly swung round, became indistinct, was seen as a ghost for a second perhaps, as an eddy of faintly glittering brass and ivory; and it was gone—vanished![2]

In a sense, studying the Bible is like entering a time machine. We must cross the barriers of time, language, culture and geography in order to understand the people of the Bible and the problems they were facing. This helps us grasp how God's Word applied to *their* situation.

Then, when we have understood how God's Word applied to the people of that century, we re-enter the time machine and return to the twentieth century. Now we are able to reflect on what we have learned and how it applies to our time and culture and the problems *we* face.

Our time machine is constructed from the various tools available to the modern student of the Bible. With these tools we can cross the barriers which separate us from the biblical world.

1. *Crossing the time barrier.* The events described

in the Bible took place thousands of years ago. This creates one obvious problem for understanding these events—*we weren't there!* Therefore, we often lack important information regarding the historical context in which these events took place.

For example, almost every New Testament letter was written to address a particular problem or set of problems: the Galatians were seeking to be justified by law; the Corinthians wanted answers to questions about marriage, spiritual gifts, meat offered to idols and so on; Timothy needed to know how to restore order to a church.

Unless we understand these problems or questions, the letters are like listening to one end of a telephone conversation. We hear what the author is saying, but we don't know *why* he is saying it. The same is true when we read the Psalms and Prophets. We know only half of the story!

One way to learn about the historical context is to look for clues within the book or passage itself. For example, in 1 John we read, "I am writing these things to you about those who are trying to lead you astray" (2:26). As we look elsewhere in the letter we discover that these false teachers had originally been part of the church: "They went out from us, but they did not really belong to us" (2:19). John calls them "antichrists" (2:18). There are many other statements, some explicit and some implicit, which give us additional details about the situation that John's readers faced and why he wrote to them.

Once we have looked within the book or passage itself, it is helpful to consult a Bible dictionary or handbook.[3] For example, under the listing "John, Epistles of" we can find further information about the historical context and purpose of 1 John.

It is also a good idea to read related passages in the Bible. For example, Psalm 51 was written by David after his adultery with Bathsheba. We can read about David and Bathsheba in 2 Samuel 11—12. (In Psalm 51 the heading over the psalm tells us why it was written. When such information isn't given, a Bible dictionary or commentary will often mention related passages.) Similarly, if we study the book of Philippians, we will want to consult the book of Acts, which provides information about the founding of the church at Philippi (Acts 16).

The more we know about the historical context of a biblical passage, the better equipped we will be to understand the message of the author. Such information can be like finding missing pieces of a puzzle. As they are put into place, the whole picture becomes much clearer.

2. *Crossing the language barrier.* The fact that the Bible was written in Hebrew, Aramaic and Greek instead of English creates a significant barrier to understanding its message. Anyone who tries to learn these languages quickly realizes how difficult they are to master. Fortunately, those who are experts in biblical languages have crossed this barrier for us (for the most part) by translating the biblical languages into modern English. In fact, there are numerous Bible translations to choose from.

There are literal translations such as the New American Standard Bible and the Revised Standard Version. There are dynamic-equivalence translations such as the New International Version, the New English Bible and the Good News Bible. And there are free translations such as the Living Bible and the New Testament in Modern English (J. B. Phillips).

Each type of translation has strengths and weaknesses. A literal translation follows the wording of Hebrew or Greek as closely as possible, but such wording often sounds awkward in English.

A free translation is more concerned with clarity than exact wording. Such translations are easy to read but give the impression that the Bible was written in the twentieth century. For example, the word *lamp* might be translated as "flashlight"!

Dynamic-equivalence translations are probably the best choice. They don't try to update matters of history or culture (a lamp is a lamp, not a flashlight). But they translate the biblical words and phrases into precise equivalents in English. As a result they are accurate and easy to read.

The smart Bible student will take advantage of all three types of translations. Each one provides unique insights into what the author originally said in his own language.

It is best, however, to use either literal or dynamic-equivalence translations such as the NIV, RSV and NASB as the basis of our study. These translations allow us to interpret the passage on our own rather than doing much of the work for us. Then, after we have grasped the basic meaning of the passage, a free translation can help to further clarify what the author is saying.[4]

Even with a good translation there will be times when we will not understand the meaning of a word. For example, the words *justification, propitiation, reconciliation* and *redemption* are extremely important theologically but are unfamiliar to many Bible students. They are unfamiliar to us because they come from the language and culture of the biblical authors rather than from the language and culture of the twentieth century.

It is important, therefore, to look up such words in a Bible dictionary. This enables us to cross the language barrier, giving us a definition which is consistent with the meaning of the biblical author. A modern dictionary can also help explain the meaning of certain words. But modern dictionaries usually tell us what words mean today rather than what they meant in biblical times.

3. *Crossing the cultural barrier.* The events in the Bible took place in many different cultures: Egyptian, Canaanite, Babylonian, Jewish, Greek and Roman (to name a few). It is not uncommon, therefore, to read about customs or beliefs that seem strange to us since they are so far removed

from twentieth-century culture.

For example, why did Rachel steal her father's household gods (Gen 31:19)? Why was Jonah so fearful of the Ninevites? Who were the Samaritans, and why was there such hatred between them and the Jews (Jn 4:9)? What was the city of Corinth like, and what special temptations did the Corinthians face because they lived there? As we come to understand the answers to such questions, we receive new insight into the passage or book we are studying.

Imagine we are studying Amos and we come across the following verse: "On the day I punish Israel for her sins . . . the horns of the altar will be cut off and fall to the ground" (Amos 3:14). This verse is meaningless to us in the twentieth century, but a Bible dictionary or encyclopedia will help us understand what Amos meant. If we look up the word *altar* or *horn*, we discover that in Old Testament times many Jews believed the altar was a place of refuge. Both Adonijah and Joab took hold of the horns of the altar for protection (1 Kings 1:50; 2:28). Amos is warning that the Israelites will flee to the altar and find its horns (that is, their protection) are gone!

We can also discover a great deal about the culture simply from the book or passage being studied. For example, the Gospels are full of references to life in first-century Palestine. We know that the Jews were under Roman rule (Lk 3:1) and expected the Messiah to come and free them from their enemies (Lk 1:71). We read about the legalism and externalism of the religious authorities and how they hindered a true knowledge of God (Mt 23). We also gain an understanding of everyday life in Bible times: business practices (Lk 16:1-18), weddings (Jn 2), funerals (Jn 11), wages (Mt 20:1-16), taxes (Mt 22:15-22) and so on. It is impossible to study the Bible without becoming immersed in ancient Middle Eastern culture. As we become more familiar with this culture, we are better able to cross this barrier between our world and theirs.

4. *Crossing the geographical barrier.* Some people are fortunate enough to visit the Holy Land. When they return, they report that the Bible comes to life in ways they have never experienced. Those of us who have not visited the Holy Land can also have this experience in a more limited way. As we learn about biblical geog-

raphy, many Bible passages take on new meaning.

For example, in Amos 1:3—2:16 the prophet condemns Damascus, Gaza, Tyre, Edom, Ammon, Moab, Judah and Israel. At first it may seem that Amos mentions these cities and nations at random, but a closer examination reveals otherwise. The first three are the capitals of heathen nations unrelated to Israel. The next three are blood relatives of Israel. Judah, the seventh, is Israel's brother nation to the south. Finally, Israel itself is named.

The effect on Amos's audience would have been staggering. The Israelites would have cheered at his judgments against the heathen nations. But as his words came closer and closer to home—Ammon, Moab, Judah—they would have begun to sweat. With the words, "For three sins of Israel, even for four, I will not turn back my wrath," they were caught in Amos's "coil of condemnation."

There are several ways to become familiar with biblical geography. Many Bibles include maps for the reader to consult. A good Bible atlas or a Bible dictionary can also supply valuable information about unfamiliar places.[5] These sources can help us trace the route of the Exodus, show us the cities conquered by Joshua and identify Israel's neighboring enemies. They can allow us to follow the ministry of Jesus and the missionary journeys of Paul. We can learn the location of the New Testament churches and how their setting may have influenced their life and culture. If we consult these sources whenever we come across an unfamiliar location in the Bible, they can help us cross the geographical barrier.

Step Two: Learning to Read
Imagine that you have entered the time machine and have completely crossed the barriers of time, language, culture and geography. You are in Corinth in the first century. You are dressed in Greek clothes. You speak Greek fluently and know the surrounding culture and geography. You are even a member of the church at Corinth and are intimately acquainted with the people and problems in the church.

As you are gathering for worship in a nearby home, a messenger comes to the door with a letter from Paul, the letter we now call 1 Corinthians. You unroll the scroll and begin reading the letter (in Greek, of course!). Does the fact that you have successfully crossed the barriers of time, language, culture and geography mean that you will automatically understand what Paul is saying? Not necessarily.

The apostle Peter was one of Paul's contemporaries and still found some things in his letters "hard to understand" (2 Pet 3:16). Of course Peter's difficulty may have been that Paul was unclear in places. But even when Paul writes clearly, our success in understanding him (or any other author) will depend on how skillful we are at reading. One aspect, therefore, of learning how to study the Bible focuses on acquiring reading skills—the kinds of skills that will help us whether we are reading the Bible, a novel, a magazine or a newspaper.

In order to read with understanding, we need to concentrate on answering one primary question: What did the author mean to convey to his original readers? (The question of what the passage means to us today will be covered in the section "Returning to the Present," p. 27.) You can discover the meaning of the author by following five guidelines:

☐ Identify the type of literature you are studying.
☐ Get an overview of the book.
☐ Study the book passage by passage.
☐ Be sensitive to the mood of the book or passage.
☐ Compare your interpretation with one or two good commentaries.

1. *Identify the type of literature you are studying.* A cult expert was giving a lecture one evening on Mormonism. A few Mormons heard about the lecture and decided to attend. About halfway through the meeting, one of them stood up and began arguing that God the Father has a physical body like ours. He "proved" his point by quoting passages which refer to God's "right arm," "hand," "eyes" and so on. The cult expert asked him to read aloud Psalm 17:8. "Hide me in the shadow of your wings."

"But that is simply a figure of speech," protested the Mormon.

"Exactly!" replied the speaker.

The biblical authors communicated in a variety of ways—through stories, letters, poems, proverbs, parables, metaphors and symbols. Each type of literature has its own unique features. We must identify the type of literature and language an author is using in order to correctly interpret his meaning. If we assume he is speaking literally when he is speaking metaphorically (the mistake made by the Mormon), we end up with nonsense.

The literature of the Bible has been classified into various types. These include:

Discourse. Discourse is a logical and extended discussion of a subject. The New Testament epistles are the clearest examples of discourse. Some of the prophetic sermons and the longer sermons of Jesus also fall into this category.

Prose narrative. This is the style used in books such as Genesis, Joshua and the Gospels. The author describes and re-creates scenes and events from biblical history that are theologically significant.

Poetry. The Psalms, of course, fit into this category. Biblical poetry uses figurative language, different types of parallelism and is emotional in nature.

Proverbs. Proverbs, such as those in the book of Proverbs, are wise sayings. They are practical *principles* for living. They should not be confused with commands or promises.

Parables. Jesus used parables more than anyone else in Scripture. A parable explains a spiritual truth by means of a story or analogy. It is an extended simile or metaphor.

Prophetic literature. The prophetic books include the four major prophets (Isaiah, Jeremiah, Ezekiel and Daniel) and the twelve minor prophets (Hosea, Joel and Amos through Malachi). The prophets were spokesmen for God who announced the curses and blessings associated with God's covenant with Israel.

Apocalyptic literature. The books of Daniel and Revelation are a special type of prophecy known as apocalyptic literature. The word *apocalypse* means to "uncover" or "reveal" something which is hidden. One distinct feature of these books is their heavy use of symbols.

Once you have identified the type of literature you are studying, consult a Bible dictionary. (If you haven't caught on by now, a Bible dictionary is a valuable tool to own.) For example, if you are studying the Psalms, it would be wise to read an article on Hebrew poetry in order to learn how it is put together. Likewise, if you are studying Revelation, read an article on apocalyptic literature. It will explain why this kind of literature seems so strange to us and will offer suggestions for interpreting it correctly.

2. *Get an overview of the book.* On a large wind-swept plain in Peru, archaeologists discovered a vast series of strange lines covering an area thirty-seven miles long. The archaeologists first thought these lines were ancient roads. Their true significance was not discovered until the men flew over the area in an airplane. The lines joined to form a design, an immense mural that could only be seen from high above.

An overview helps us discover the meaning of an author in two ways. First, it enables us to discover the main *theme* of the book as we observe repeated ideas. For example, the author of Hebrews emphasizes Christ's superiority. "So he became as much superior to the angels as the name he has inherited is superior to theirs" (1:4). "Jesus has been found worthy of greater honor than Moses" (3:3). "We have a great high priest" (4:14).

Second, an overview helps us discover the *structure* of the book—how the parts of the book contribute to the overall theme. The structure of Hebrews clearly demonstrates the superiority of Christ:

a. Christ is superior to the prophets (1:1-3).
b. Christ is superior to the angels (1:4—2:18).
c. Christ is superior to Moses (3:1—4:13).
d. Christ is superior to Aaron (4:14—10:18).
e. Christ is superior as the new and living way to God (10:19—12:29).

The structure of a book will be closely related to its literary type. An epistle such as Hebrews is organized around ideas. Historical narratives can be structured in a variety of ways: Genesis (after chapter 11) is organized around people (Abraham, Isaac, Jacob and Joseph); Exodus is structured around geographical locations and events (in Egypt, en route to Sinai and at Sinai). The poetry of Psalm 119 is structured around the letters of the Hebrew alphabet!

The theme and structure of a book are the author's tools for accomplishing his *purpose* (see the section "Crossing the time barrier," p. 7). For example, because the "Hebrews" were being persecuted for their faith in Christ, they were tempted to forsake Christianity and return to Judaism. The author emphasizes how foolish and serious this would be since Christ is far superior to anyone or anything Judaism offered.

An overview is like looking through a zoom lens. Begin with a panoramic view through the lens by reading quickly through the book, trying to discover repeated ideas or words that tie the book together. When it isn't possible to read the entire book, skim through its contents, paying particular attention to chapter or paragraph headings in your Bible.

Next zoom in closer by looking for major sections or divisions within the book. Each section will focus primarily on one subject. Once you have discovered that subject, try to summarize it by giving a brief title to the section. Now you are ready to focus on the details of the landscape— the paragraphs, sentences and words.

At each step of the way look for connections or relationships between the sections and paragraphs. For instance, if we were studying Romans, we would find that 1:18—3:20 describes the *need* of humanity; then 3:21—5:21 shows God's *solution* to that need. Romans 7:7—8:39 contrasts the *death* that comes through sin (7:7-25) with the *life* that comes through Christ and his Spirit (8:1-39).

As an author progresses from one paragraph or section to another, he might move from problem to solution, cause to effect, general to specific. He may use comparison, contrast, repetition and so on. We can become alert to these links in his chain of reasoning by asking ourselves how each section relates to the next and how it contributes to the overall argument of the author.

The more times we read a book, the more familiar we will become with its theme and structure. Our original overview will help us to understand the whole of the book. This understanding will tend to affect the way we interpret its parts. But as we gain familiarity with the parts, our understanding of the whole may need to be modified, and so on. Each time we go through this cycle, we will come closer and closer to grasping the meaning of the author.

3. *Study the book passage by passage.* Once you have an overview of the theme and structure of a book, begin studying it passage by passage. In our modern Bibles a passage can be a paragraph, a group of paragraphs or a chapter. Realize, however, that the Bible did not originally contain chapters, paragraphs or verses (or even punctua-

tion!). These are helpful additions to our Bibles, but we need not be bound by them.

As we study a passage, we should seek to understand its content and its context.

We discover the *content* of a passage by reading and rereading it. As we read we must ask ourselves, "What is the main subject of the passage?"

For example, love is obviously the subject of 1 Corinthians 13 since the word (or pronouns referring to it) occurs seventeen times in only thirteen verses. But love is a broad subject, one which Paul might have looked at from a hundred different perspectives.

Therefore, we must also ask, "What did Paul say about love?" A closer look at the chapter reveals the following:

a. Love is superior to spiritual gifts because without love all gifts are meaningless (13:1-3).

b. Love is superior to spiritual gifts because of its selfless qualities (vv. 4-7).

c. Love is superior to spiritual gifts because it endures forever (vv. 8-13).

We discover the *context* of the passage by reading the verses or paragraphs immediately before and after it. As we read we must ask ourselves,

"Why is this passage here? How does the author use it to make his point clearer?"

Many people, for example, read 1 Corinthians 13 without considering how it fits into Paul's over-all argument. We find it is sandwiched between two chapters which talk about spiritual gifts. Therefore, Paul's discussion of love *in this context* must have something to do with the broader sub-ject of gifts, as the outline above clearly indicates.

4. *Be sensitive to the mood of the book or passage.* The Bible is more than a collection of ideas. The biblical authors and characters were people like us with passions and feelings. Sorrow and agony permeate Jesus' experience in Gethsemane. Gala-tians radiates the heat of Paul's anger toward the Judaizers and his perplexity over the Galatians. Psalm 148 is bursting with praise. While this is a more subjective aspect of Bible study, it can give us rich insights into the feelings and motivations of the biblical authors or characters. This in turn will add depth to our understanding of what they are saying.

5. *Compare your interpretation with one or two com-mentaries.* Once you feel you have understood the main subject of the passage and what the author

is saying about it, compare your interpretation with that of one or two good commentaries.[6] They can give you additional insights which you might have missed and can serve as a corrective if you have misunderstood something the author has said. But do your best to understand the passage on your own before consulting commentaries.

Step Three: Returning to the Present

Now we are ready to re-enter the time machine and return to the twentieth century. As we travel from the biblical world back to our own, we will seek to apply God's Word to the needs and problems of our time and culture, using language that is meaningful to us today.

The eternal nature of Scripture should cause us to apply the Bible *carefully* and *prayerfully*.

In 2 Timothy 2:7 Paul writes to his young associate: "Think over what I say, for the Lord will grant you understanding in everything" (RSV). Notice the two halves of this verse. First, Paul exhorts Timothy to *think* about what he has said. Studying and applying the Bible requires thought and reflection. We should handle the Scriptures carefully, using all of the tools and resources God has given us for understanding his Word. Only then can we be confident that we are applying the Scriptures in the way God intends. If we rush through our Bible study, we may end up hanging an applicational elephant from an interpretive thread.

Second, Paul tells Timothy it is the Lord who grants understanding. Therefore, we must also handle the Bible prayerfully, asking the Author of Scripture to grant us understanding in everything. He must open our eyes to see clearly what he is saying. He must reveal those areas of our lives that need to be transformed by his Word and his Spirit. The psalmist realized this when he wrote, "Open my eyes that I may see wonderful things in your law" (Ps 119:18). The Lord is the revealer of Scripture.

To properly apply the Scriptures, we must remember what was said earlier about the nature of Scripture. Almost every book of the Bible was written to address specific problems, needs and questions of the people living *at that time*. For example, the Corinthians had problems of division, immorality and lawsuits among believers. They also had questions about marriage, food sacrificed to idols and spiritual gifts. Paul wrote 1 Corinthians to address their specific problems and to answer their specific questions.

We face many of these same problems and questions today. It is still possible to take a fellow believer to court, and we still have questions about marriage. In fact, there are hundreds of ways in which our problems and needs correspond to those faced by the people in the Bible. This is natural since we share a common humanity.

This leads us to the first principle of application:

Whenever our situation corresponds to that faced by the original readers, God's Word to us is the same as it was to them.

But there are also situations from ancient times that do not have an exact counterpart today. This, too, is to be expected because of the differences between modern and biblical cultures. For example, no one in our society sacrifices food to idols.

In such cases we should follow the second principle of application:

Whenever our situation does not correspond to that faced by the original readers, we should look for the principle *underlying God's Word to them. We can then apply that principle to comparable situations today.*[7]

What was the principle underlying Paul's words about food sacrificed to idols? He was concerned that the Corinthians not do anything that would lead someone with a weak conscience to sin: "Therefore, if what I eat causes my brother to fall into sin, I will never eat meat again, so that I will not cause him to fall" (1 Cor 8:13). This principle might be applied to many situations today, such as whether a Christian should drink alcoholic beverages around someone who is a former alcoholic—or whether to drink at all.

Once we understand these principles of application, we will find unlimited ways in which God's Word applies today. We can ask such questions as:

☐ Is there a command for me to obey?

☐ Is there a promise to claim?

☐ Is there an example to follow?

☐ Is there a sin to avoid or confess?

☐ Is there a reason for thanksgiving or praise?

☐ What does this passage teach me about God, Jesus Christ, myself, others?

Practice Makes Perfect (Well, Almost)

Learning to study the Bible is like learning any other skill—the more we do it, the easier it becomes. At first, following the steps outlined in this booklet may seem mechanical, like learning how to type. But after a while, many of these steps will seem much more natural, almost automatic. And remember, we are not alone in Bible study. The Holy Spirit did not write Scripture in order to confuse us. He will help us understand and apply the Bible as we pray, study diligently and make use of many of the study aids available today. Bon appetit!

Jack Kuhatschek is executive vice president and publisher at Baker Publishing Group and the author of many Bible study guides and books, including Applying the Bible.

Notes

[1] As quoted by Robert A. Traina, *Methodical Bible Study* (Wilmore, Ky.: Asbury Theological Seminary, 1952), pp. 97-98.

[2] H. G. Wells, *The Time Machine* (New York: Bantam Books, 1982), pp. 9-10.

[3] For a good one-volume Bible dictionary, I would recommend J. D. Douglas, ed., *New Bible Dictionary*, 2d ed. (Wheaton, Ill.: Tyndale, 1982). It contains a wealth of information.

[4] What about the King James Version? It is beautifully written, but I would not recommend it for Bible study. A good translation should cross the language barrier between the biblical world and our own. The KJV did that for those living in the seventeenth century, but for those of us today, methinks a four-hundred-year gap doth create unnecessary confusion!

[5] *The Macmillan Bible Atlas* (New York: Macmillan, 1968) is one of the best Bible atlases available.

[6] For a good, basic commentary series I would recommend *The Tyndale New Testament Commentaries* (Grand Rapids, Mich.: Eerdmans) and *The Tyndale Old Testament Commentaries* (Downers Grove, Ill.: InterVarsity Press).

[7] For a fuller discussion of the principles of application see Gordon D. Fee and Douglas Stuart, *How to Read the Bible for All Its Worth* (Grand Rapids, Mich.: Zondervan, 1982), pp. 57-71. This is also an excellent book on how to study the various types of literature in the Bible.